Schaum Fingerpower POP LEVEL THREE

10 PIANO SOLOS WITH TECHNI...M-UPS

Arrar ...EAT

The purpose of the Fingerpower Pop series is to provide musical experiences beyond the traditional **Fingerpower®** books. The series offers students a variety of popular tunes, including hits from today's pop charts as well as from classic movie themes, beloved Broadway shows, and more! The arrangements progress in order of difficulty, and technique warm-ups are included for each solo.

CONTENTS

ISBN 978-1-5400-3480-9

EXCLUSIVELY DISTRIBUTED BY
HAL•LEONARD®

Visit Hal Leonard Online at
www.halleonard.com

Contact us:
Hal Leonard
7777 West Bluemound Road
Milwaukee, WI 53213
Email: info@halleonard.com

In Europe, contact:
Hal Leonard Europe Limited
42 Wigmore Street
Marylebone, London, W1U 2RN
Email: info@halleonardeurope.com

In Australia, contact:
Hal Leonard Australia Pty. Ltd.
4 Lentara Court
Cheltenham, Victoria, 3192 Australia
Email: info@halleonard.com.au

WARM-UPS

Warm-Up for
"Gravity Falls"
(page 10)

BROKEN & BLOCKED CHORDS in D MINOR
Use fingers 5, 3, 1 (L.H.) and fingers 1, 3, 5 (R.H.) except where marked.

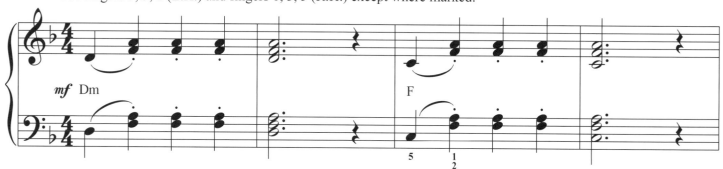

Warm-Up for
"Set Fire to the Rain"
(page 12)

LEGATO 3rds

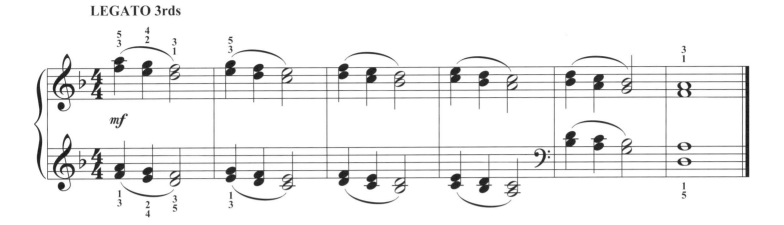

Warm-Ups for
"Hey Jude"
(page 14)

1. SCALES ON TONIC & DOMINANT, F MAJOR

2. PRIMARY CHORDS in F MAJOR

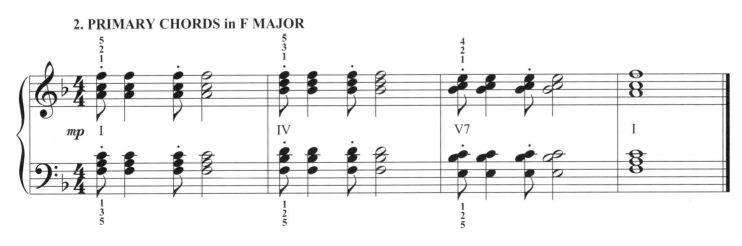

Warm-Ups for
"Jurassic Park"
(page 16)

1. INVERSIONS OF PRIMARY CHORDS in B-FLAT MAJOR
Use fingers 5, 3, 1 (L.H.) and fingers 1, 3, 5 (R.H.) except where marked.

2. B-FLAT SCALE in 6ths
Use fingers 1 and 5 throughout.

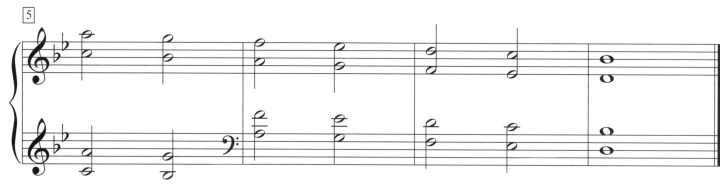

Warm-Up for
"I Dreamed a Dream"
(page 18)

PENTASCALES with DOTTED RHYTHM

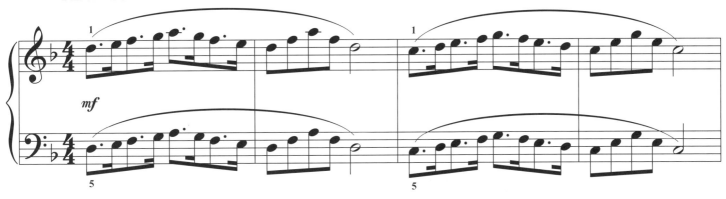

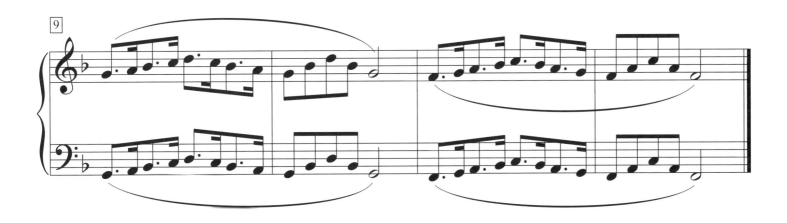

Warm-Up for
"Beauty and the Beast"
(page 20)

DIATONIC ARPEGGIOS in C MAJOR
Practice with and without pedal.

Warm-Up for
"The Fox"
(page 22)

VOICES OF THE FOX
Keep the lower voice as legato as possible.

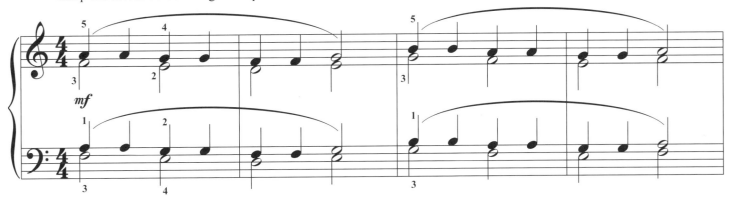

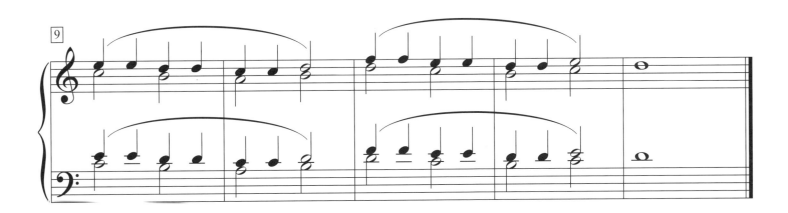

8

Warm-Ups for
"River Flows in You"
(page 24)

1. FOCUS ON WEAKER FINGERS OF THE RIGHT HAND—16th NOTES

2. FOCUS ON WEAKER FINGERS—8th NOTES

Warm-Up for
"Dear Theodosia"
(page 26)

LEFT-HAND OSTINATO
Practice with or without pedal.

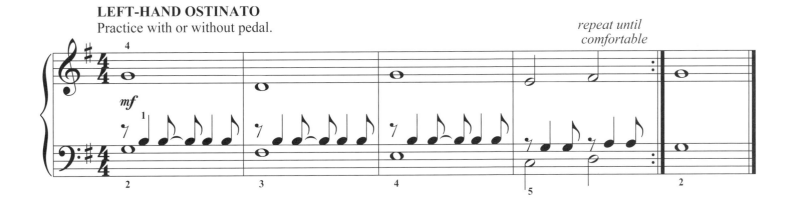

Warm-Up for
"Say Something"
(page 29)

BLOCKED & BROKEN CHORDS in D MAJOR
Practice legato with and without pedal.

SOLOS

Gravity Falls
(Main Theme)

By Brad Breeck
Arranged by James Poteat

WARM-UP: page 2

Set Fire to the Rain

Words and Music by Adele Adkins
and Fraser Smith
Arranged by James Poteat

WARM-UP: page 3

Driving ♩ = c. 108

Hey Jude

Words and Music by John Lennon
and Paul McCartney
Arranged by James Poteat

WARM-UPS: page 3

Relaxed ♩ = c. 60

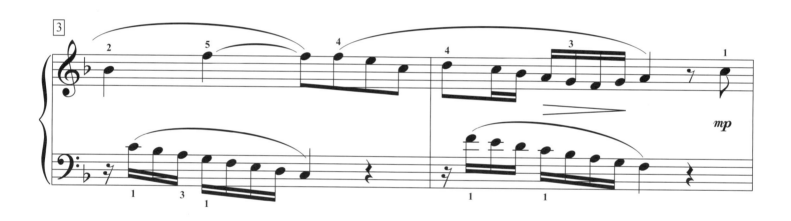

Theme from
"Jurassic Park"
from the Universal Motion Picture JURASSIC PARK

Composed by John Williams
Arranged by James Poteat

WARM-UPS: page 4

I Dreamed a Dream
from LES MISÉRABLES

Music by Claude-Michel Schönberg
Lyrics by Alain Boublil,
Jean-Marc Natel and Herbert Kretzmer
Arranged by James Poteat

WARM-UP: page 5

With resolve ♩ = c. 64

Beauty and the Beast
from BEAUTY AND THE BEAST

Music by Alan Menken
Lyrics by Howard Ashman
Arranged by James Poteat

WARM-UP: page 6

The Fox

Words and Music by Tor Hermansen,
Mikkel Eriksen, Baard Ylvisaaker, Vegard Ylvisaaker,
Christian Lochstoer and Nicholas Boundy
Arranged by James Poteat

WARM-UP: page 7

Scampering ♩ = c. 124

River Flows in You

By Yiruma
Arranged by James Poteat

WARM-UPS: page 8

Dear Theodosia

Words and Music by
Lin-Manuel Miranda
Arranged by James Poteat

WARM-UP: page 9

Tenderly ♩ = c. 104

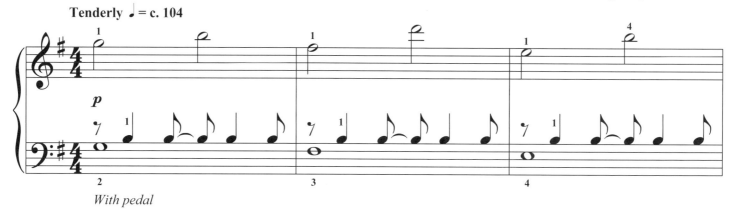

With pedal

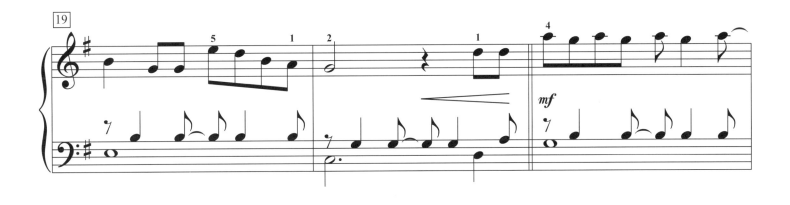

28

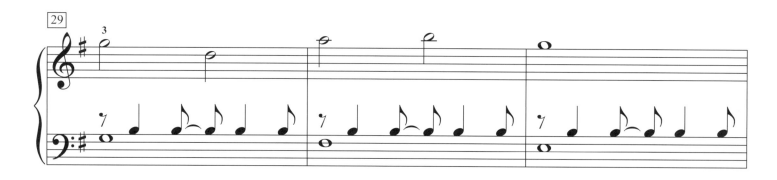

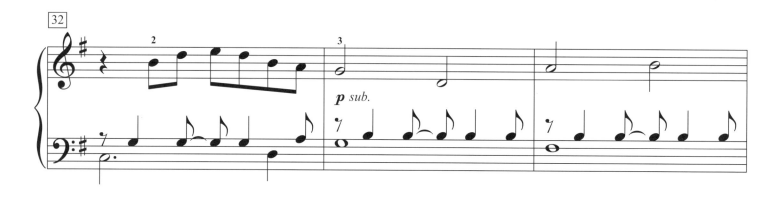

Say Something

Words and Music by Ian Axel,
Chad Vaccarino and Mike Campbell
Arranged by James Poteat

WARM-UP: page 9

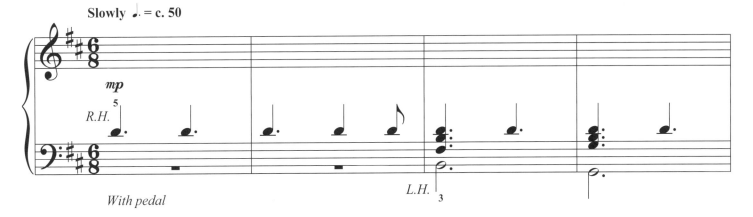

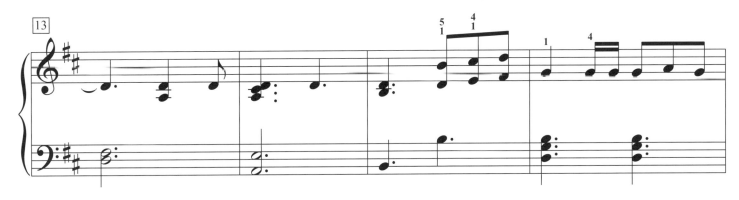

ABOUT THE ARRANGER

Since 2007 **James Poteat** has taught piano, trombone, euphonium, music theory, and composition in Woodstock, Georgia. Mr. Poteat works with students of all ages and skill levels and is equally comfortable in the worlds of popular and classical music. James is constantly arranging music for his students and is dedicated to creating and using materials of the highest quality. Learn more about James and his work by visiting **www.musicalintentions.com**.